BRITAIN IN OLD PHOTOGRAPHS

LETCHWORTH GARDEN CITY

ROBERT LANCASTER

ALAN SUTTON PUBLISHING LIMITED

Alan Sutton Publishing Limited
Phoenix Mill · Far Thrupp · Stroud
Gloucestershire · GL5 2BU

FIRST GARDEN CITY
HERITAGE MUSEUM

First published 1995

Cover photographs: front: Leys Avenue,
c. 1928; *back*: a works' trip to Bedfordshire,
1906. *Page 1*: Mr Bullmore's children, 1909.

British Library Cataloguing in Publication Data.
A catalogue record for this book is available from
the British Library.

ISBN 0-7509-1113-1

Typeset in 9/10 Sabon.
Typesetting and origination by
Alan Sutton Publishing Limited.
Printed in Great Britain by
Ebenezer Baylis, Worcester.

Children enjoying the swing-boats on the Arena in the early 1950s. In the background can be seen the Palace Cinema and the fire station. Both buildings were demolished in the mid-1980s.

Contents

Acknowledgements 4

Introduction 5

1. Building the Garden City 7

2. The Cheap Cottages Exhibition of 1905 and 1907 13

3. Living in the Garden City 19

4. The Letchworth Jubilee Fair of Industry and Trade, 1953 37

5. Places of Worship 45

6. The Garden City at War 49

7. The Best Days of Your Life 57

8. Industry and Commerce 63

9. 'Pull Yourselves Together Girls': The Spirella Company, 1910–89 85

10. Garden City Scenes 95

Acknowledgements

I should like to thank the many people who have given or loaned to the First Garden City Heritage Museum the photographs and postcards that are reproduced in this book. The original photographs were skilfully copied by Peter Davies of Peter Davies Photography. Special thanks are due to Mitzi Blacklaws, who typed the manuscript, and to Liz Cummings and Christine Webb, who read, criticized, mostly kindly, and corrected the copy.

Girls from the Spirella factory enjoying a snowball fight on Norton Common in 1919.

Introduction

Letchworth Garden City is the world's first garden city and was built as a social experiment inspired by the founder of the garden city movement, Ebenezer Howard. Howard believed that 'Town and Country must be married and out of this joyous union will spring a new hope, a new life, a new civilization'. The combination of town and country would, Howard believed, solve two of the major problems of the late nineteenth century, which were the uncontrolled growth of towns and the depopulation of the countryside. Garden cities should be built to have all the benefits of town life and of country life, with the disadvantages of neither. They would be built by private enterprise and profits would be used to improve the garden city itself.

Letchworth Garden City was founded in 1903 and was designed to be an industrial town. It would have a population of about 32,000 inhabitants, who would come from a variety of social backgrounds. It would be free from overcrowding, slum housing and pollution. The countryside would be brought into the town by providing parks and open spaces, low density housing and extensive landscaping.

For many years the development of Letchworth Garden City was held back by lack of capital. The development company First Garden City Limited had considerable difficulties in the early years encouraging companies to relocate to the Garden City. There was a publicity and marketing triumph in 1905, however, when the Cheap Cottages Exhibition was held in the Garden City. The intention was to show that it was possible to build low-cost housing for rural labourers using low-cost materials. This event, which attracted 80,000 visitors and attained nationwide publicity, put Letchworth Garden City firmly on the map.

From this point development proceeded fairly steadily until 1960 when First Garden City Limited was taken over by a property company, Hotel York. One of Hotel York's motives was asset stripping, something fiercely resisted by Letchworth Urban District Council who succeeded in promoting a Private Member's Bill through Parliament. This dissolved First Garden City Limited and created in its place a public authority, namely Letchworth Garden City Corporation. The role of the corporation was to manage and develop the Garden City estate and use the profits for the benefit of the residents.

The corporation continued to do this until 1 October 1995 when it was replaced by Letchworth Garden City Heritage Foundation, an Industrial and Provident Society with specific charitable aims. The Heritage Foundation will continue to manage the Garden City estate for the benefit of the Letchworth community.

The photographs in this book date from 1904 to 1995 and show many aspects of Garden City life, from industry and commerce to sport and recreation. I hope that readers enjoy looking at them as much as I have enjoyed selecting them. The photographs are the copyright of the First Garden City Heritage Museum, a Letchworth Garden City Heritage Foundation Enterprise.

Robert Lancaster
Curator
First Garden City
Heritage Museum

Fred Nott's bakers delivery vans on the Arena, c. 1950.

BUILDING THE GARDEN CITY

Early in 1904 numbers of unemployed workmen were brought to Letchworth Garden City to build the roads, drains and sewers. They were housed in wood huts known as the 'black sheds' in Nevells Road. Today the site is occupied by the police station.

The workmen mainly came from London and were employed for continuous periods of one month, which could be extended. Allowances up to a maximum of 17s 6d per week were paid to families who remained in London. The men received board and lodging plus 6d per week for incidental expenses. Rules included prompt obedience to orders, sobriety and the observance of appointed hours.

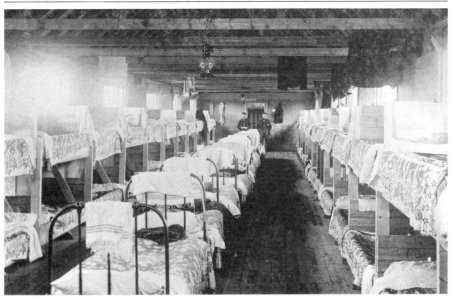

Accommodation for the workmen was basic and divided into sleeping rooms, a mess room, kitchen, lavatories and bathrooms.

This is the kitchen after a meal. Milk was collected in churns from Auburn's dairy at Wilbury Farm. Millicent Auburn, daughter of William Auburn the farmer, was given a parrot called Cocky by one of the foremen. This parrot, obviously rather confused, would roost with the hens.

The first houses to be built on the Garden City estate were a small group called Alpha Cottages on Baldock Road. They were built by Picton and Hope and were finished in 1904. Here we can see one nearly completed block with the proud workmen posing for the camera.

The railway sidings were an early and most important facility to be developed. Building materials, including roof tiles as seen in the photograph, were brought in by goods train together with raw materials for the factories. Finished products were usually distributed by train.

The residents of Eastholm and Eastholm Green posing outside one of the houses. This development was built in 1905 and 1906 for the Garden City Tenants and a model of the scheme is proudly displayed.

Particulars of Eight Houses

now in course of erection on

COWSLIP HILL, LETCHWORTH

Excellent Position.   Near Letchworth Station, Buses and Shops

Prices £590 - £635

INCLUDING LEGAL COSTS OF LEASE

Best Houses,
Good Sites,
Nice
Designs,
Careful
Work,
Sound
Materials.

TYPE "E"   TYPE "F"

Homes of Character

THE houses have been designed as a group, distinctive in character, modern in design, attractive in appearance. Real homes, combining modern building practice and modern convenience at their best.

FOR FURTHER PARTICULARS APPLY TO

J. L. A. WHITE, A.B.I.C.C., Builder, Bridge Rd., Letchworth

Phone 295

15/7/37.

In 1937 you could buy one of these very desirable semi-detached houses in Cowslip Hill for between £590 and £635. This style of house was very popular in the 1930s.

THE CHEAP COTTAGES EXHIBITIONS
OF 1905 AND 1907

The Nook Cottage, No. 2 Cross Street, was built as Exhibit 59 in the 1905 Cheap Cottages Exhibition. The architect was George E. Clare and the builder was Chas R. Price. It was constructed in two months from breeze concrete on a lattice framework with Mack fire and vermin-proof slabs. The cottage was designed to be used by labourers in rural districts.

One of eight concrete cottages built for the exhibition was Exhibit 58, No. 4 Cross Street. It was built from concrete blocks by the Concrete Machinery Company Limited of Liverpool. The blocks were cast on site by the company's portable 'Pioneer' hand-power machine, which had a minimum capacity of 150 blocks a day. The cost was £150. This cottage won first prize for the best cottage built of cement concrete.

Another concrete entry in the 1905 competition was this house, No. 158 Wilbury Road. This exhibit was constructed of prefabricated concrete slabs cast in Liverpool, transported by train to Letchworth and erected in 36 hours.

One of the most unusual exhibits in the 1905 Cheap Cottages Exhibition was 'The Round House'. This was designed by Hesketh and Stokes for Cubitts and was constructed of prefabricated reinforced concrete panels to form a 16-sided structure. The panels were cast on site, as can be seen from the photograph.

'The Round House' was built to demonstrate the use of prefabricated concrete and was not intended to be lived in. However, the building was occupied up to the mid-1980s. By 1986, the structure had deteriorated to such an extent that the family had to move out and the building disintegrated in 1987.

This 1905 'Cheap Cottage', No. 222 Nevells Road, was built at a cost of £150 in six weeks by the British Uralite Company Limited. It was constructed of Uralite Kent Board, an asbestos-based, man-made material. The architect was Frederick Wheeler and Son, who designed the cottage to be cool in summer and warm in winter. One advantage of this method of construction was that the residents could move in immediately after building work had finished.

In 1907 Letchworth Garden City hosted an Urban Cottages and Smallholdings Exhibition. The site of the smallholdings section was Baldock Road and Nos 97 and 99 Baldock Road, Exhibits 270 and 271, can be seen in the centre of the photograph with their outbuildings.

LIVING IN THE GARDEN CITY

Afternoon tea at No. 54 Common View, *c.* 1909. The 1909 Directory lists a T. Williams as resident at this address.

Afternoon tea again but this time on the veranda of Zabell House, No. 341 Norton Way South. The Misses H. and K. Underwood lived here from about 1907. Miss Hannah Underwood is listed as living at this address in the 1948 Directory but there is no reference to her after this date.

Music was an important part of the social life of the Garden City. This is the First Garden City Military Band posing outside the Letchworth Refreshment Rooms, Station Road, about 1912. This building had been demolished by the 1920s.

A bazaar at the Mrs Howard Memorial Hall, possibly the one held on 27–9 November 1907 to liquidate the debt on the hall. The sum of £174 was raised, clearing the debt.

May Day celebrations were an important feature in the Garden City calendar. This is the 1922 Norton School May Day, with May Queen Lily Wheeler sitting on the right and Mary Cook, the previous year's May Queen, to the left. The celebration was held on Westholm.

More 'Games For May' with the children of Hillshott School in 1933. The May Queen was Joan Lilley. This was the first year that Hillshott School used a gramophone in its celebrations.

Pixmore School also celebrated May Day. The date this photograph was taken is thought to be about 1916.

The scene is Broadway and the occasion is a hospital fair in 1935.

An anonymous lady and anonymous goat with The Cloisters in the background. This photograph was taken in about 1907 or 1908 and shows how isolated The Cloisters was until residential development engulfed it from the 1920s onwards. The Cloisters was built as a centre for theosophical meditation in 1905 for Miss Annie Lawrence and was later used for outdoor Sunday concerts until the outbreak of the Second World War in 1939.

The sun did not always shine on Letchworth Garden City. Here a splendid and frenzied snowball fight is in full swing on Broadway in the 1930s. Just visible in the background is the Boys' Club and the police station.

The Garden City Naturalists' Society was founded on 30 April 1908 in the Mrs Howard Memorial Hall. Here we see some of the members on a field trip to Odsey House, Ashwell, on 19 June 1915.

Afternoon tea in the garden of North Holt, Norton Way North, July 1920. Taking tea are, from left to right, May Radclyffe, Mr and Mrs A.J. Johnson and nieces with F.G.P. Radclyffe. Frederick Radclyffe was one of the first residents of the Garden City, arriving on 2 October 1904. He tried smallholding but was unsuccessful and took a job with the Garden City Press. Radclyffe was a Quaker and at the outbreak of the First World War took a course of first aid and ambulance tuition. In 1915 he went to France with a Society of Friends (Quaker) ambulance unit. In 1917 he joined the motor transport section of the Army Service Corps as a driver and was posted to East Africa.

In 1912 an exciting event took place in the Garden City – that strange new invention the aeroplane came to town. An encampment was set up at Willian and two aircraft were stationed there to take part in a large-scale training exercise. Many people came to gaze with wonder on these rare contraptions.

Tragedy struck on 6 September 1912 when the second aircraft, piloted by Captain Patrick Hamilton with Lieutenant A. Wyness-Stuart as passenger, crashed at Graveley. The funeral service was held at St Saviour's Church, Hitchin, and the coffins were carried to the station through streets lined with spectators.

Later a memorial was erected on the Wymondley Road on the spot where the clothes of the dead officers are buried.

The Girls' Club banner, proudly held by two members with others, some in fancy dress, in procession behind. They are taking part in a May Day celebration and were photographed outside the First Garden City Limited estate office in Broadway. The date would be about 1920.

National Play Day was celebrated on Wednesday 2 August 1995 in Howard Park. Local children had a great time being entertained and entertaining themselves.

Keeping fit was very popular in the 1930s. Cycling, rambling and, as demonstrated here by Mr Wegmuller to an impressed group of ladies, floor exercises were all popular ways to keep fit and healthy.

Letchworth Cricket Club was formed in 1907. This is the team for 1911. Back row, left to right: H.B. Brand, J.H. Haysman, R. Doult, F.S. Jarden. Second row: R. Bloxham, A.W. Brunt (umpire), H.E. Miller, S. Cook, C.W.E. Ansell, E.E. Dennis, J.R. Haigh, J.W.F. Powell. Front row: C.J. Sorrie (Hon Secretary), H. Hankin, H. Craske (Vice-President), A. Ansell (Captain), T. Bolton (Vice-President), T. Hawes, G.H. Stephens (Vice-President).

3 SWIMMING GALA GARDEN CITY.

Letchworth's first public swimming bath, in Pixmore Way, was opened by Sir Ralph Neville at 3.15 p.m. on Saturday 27 June 1908. This was followed by a gala that started with a breast and back stroke swimming race. Next P.C. Brewer demonstrated the Monte Cristo dive. Cock-fighting on rafts followed, then a diving display, a team race between First Garden City Limited estate office, W.H. Smith and Son and Garden City Press, and a barrel race. The final of the breast and back stroke swimming race was held and to finish there was the Cap and Bells Chase.

The Pixmore swimming pool was a popular, if chilly and at times murky, facility.

The Ozone open-air swimming pool on Norton Common opened on 17 August 1935.
Fred Nott took the first plunge into the pool.

Letchworth Football Club team in the 1932/3 season. As well as Letchworth Football Club, many companies also had their own football teams.

Letchworth Fire Brigade had a series of fire-engines since it was founded in 1905. The appliance in this photograph, taken on the Arena, is a Dennis 80 h.p. model, which was acquired in 1934.

The Skittles Inn, now the Settlement, was built in Nevells Road to provide the facilities and atmosphere of a public house but it did not sell alcohol. It opened in 1907.

The opening of the billiard room at the Skittles Inn in 1907 was perceived by many as a most important event in the history of the Garden City.

As well as all the other facilities, including the bar and billiard room, the Skittles also had a tea garden.

This photograph was taken in about 1920 outside the Skittles Inn, Nevells Road. The girls on the horses are two of Bill Furmston's children. Bill Furmston was the manager of the Skittles Inn and later the People's House (see p. 120). The horses came from John Ray's building company, which was situated on the opposite side of the road.

The year 1913 was quite significant in the development of the Garden City. Not only were Pixmore School and the permanent railway station opened, but so too was the railway bridge linking Norton Way South and Norton Way North. This was an important event attended by many people. Previously pedestrians and small vehicles wanting to cross the railway had had to use the narrow bridge known as the 'Cattle Creep'. Large vehicles had to detour via Baldock.

THE LETCHWORTH JUBILEE FAIR
OF INDUSTRY AND TRADE, 1953

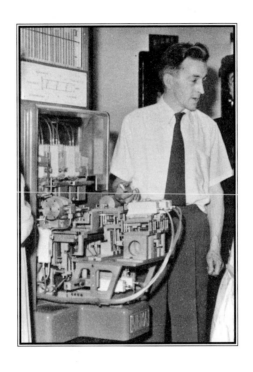

On 1 September 1953 Letchworth Garden City celebrated its fiftieth anniversary and the town enjoyed a Jubilee Week. The first event was Divine Service at the Howard Memorial, Howard Park.

There were novel competitions such as a window-dressing competition, won by the Co-op.

The main event was an industrial and trade fair held on the Arena from 1–3 September. Before the trade fair opened there were hectic preparations by the staff of First Garden City Limited.

Bob Shaw, lorryman, delivering supplies.

The Guinness Clock being lowered into position by a Kryn and Lahy crane.

Vic Miles, left, unloading a lorry.

After days of preparation Letchworth Jubilee Fair was opened at 3 p.m. on 1 September 1953.

The Hollerith electro-mechanical and electronic office machinery and equipment was shown by the British Tabulating Machine Company Limited.

There were fifty-four exhibitors' stands including Brookers, displaying hardware and furnishings.

Foster & Scott Limited, men's and boys' clothing and outfitting business. They opened in The Arcade in 1926.

Munt's displayed a selection of Raleigh and Phillips cycles and Silver Cross prams. George Munt opened his first shop in Commerce Avenue in 1910 and in 1912 moved to Eastcheap.

Sigma Instrument Company Limited displayed a range of equipment for the gas industry as well as fine measuring equipment.

Saint Paul's Amateur Dramatic Society performed a variety show each evening.

The 20,000th visitor receives a gift from Mr Ritchie of First Garden City Limited.

PLACES OF WORSHIP

On Wednesday 7 August 1907 the foundation stone of St Michael's Church in Norton Way South was laid. From Church House in Silver Birch Cottages, the procession made its way to Norton Way South.

The foundation stone laying ceremony. The foundation stone reads 'In The Faith of Jesus Christ And In The Name Of The Blessed Trinity This Stone Was Laid By The Honourary W F D Smith MP on August 7 (Feast Of The Holy Name) 1907'. Sealed beneath the foundation stone was a bottle containing newspapers, the order of service for the ceremony and three coins of 1907.

The completed St Michael's Church, seen from Howard Park. It was demolished and an office block erected on the site in the 1960s.

The Primitive Methodist Church, Broadway. The church opened in August 1914 and was demolished in the 1950s. The site was incorporated into North Hertfordshire College.

Cutting the first sods for the foundations of the Elim Church, Norton Way North, April 1925. The wooden Elim Hall in the background was built in 1923 but very quickly proved to be too small and it was decided to build a more permanent church. This was erected around the wooden Elim Hall, which was then dismantled from the inside. The new building opened in June 1927.

This is the Free Church, photographed in about 1912, which occupied the site of the present Free Church Hall in Gernon Road. The first Free Church was financed by public subscription and opened in 1905. It was later extended and finally replaced by the present church, which was built next to it in 1923–4.

Section Six

THE GARDEN CITY AT WAR

The First World War had a major impact on Letchworth Garden City, as it did on every city, town and village in the country. The spirit of optimism and the feeling that it would all be over by Christmas soon gave way to a more sombre understanding of the horrors of warfare. This initial optimism was shown by the Spirella employees, who lined the railway line to cheer and wave goodbye to the territorials, who were called to their depot at Hertford on 5 August 1914.

Not every man was prepared to fight for his country, some refusing for religious or moral reasons. These conscientious objectors were obliged or volunteered to work on the land, serve in a non-combatant or medical capacity or, in extreme cases, were imprisoned. A group of conscientious objectors was billeted at Manor Farm, Norton, where they worked on the land. One distinguished member was Herbert Morrison, who later became a Labour Party minister, seen sitting in the centre row, on the extreme left.

One young man who went to war was bugler Raymond Quin, the youngest territorial to serve in the British Army. He survived, unlike the 120 Letchworth men who died serving their country.

The invasion of Belgium in early August 1914 resulted in a flood of refugees fleeing to Holland and the British Isles. A small group came to Letchworth in late August 1914, to be followed by many others in 1915. By late 1917 there were food shortages and many areas of land were being cultivated. This photograph shows a group of Belgians, including one at the back wearing clogs, digging potatoes in 1917.

Those who died during the First World War were remembered at a solemn service held in Station Place on 12 October 1919. This was organized by the Letchworth branch of the National Federation of Discharged and Demobilized Sailors and Soldiers. The procession assembled on Norton Way South near Howard Park at 2.15 p.m. and marched via Leys Avenue to the Cenotaph in Station Place. Following the laying of wreaths (above), the procession continued to Town Square where the service was held (below).

Howard Park, September 1939. These children are evacuees from London; their gas masks are in the cardboard boxes near by.

Pixmore School pupils digging for victory during the Second World War.

One of the Letchworth Home Guard units poses outside the Country Gentleman's Association building in Icknield Way, *c.* 1944.

Italian prisoners of war, April 1945. Their camp was at Royston and groups of prisoners were transported to Letchworth to work on the railway, where this photograph was taken.

During the Second World War factories frequently recruited their own fire-fighting teams. These are Irvin Airchute's fire-fighters, with Leslie Irvin standing in the centre.

Section Seven

THE BEST DAYS OF YOUR LIFE

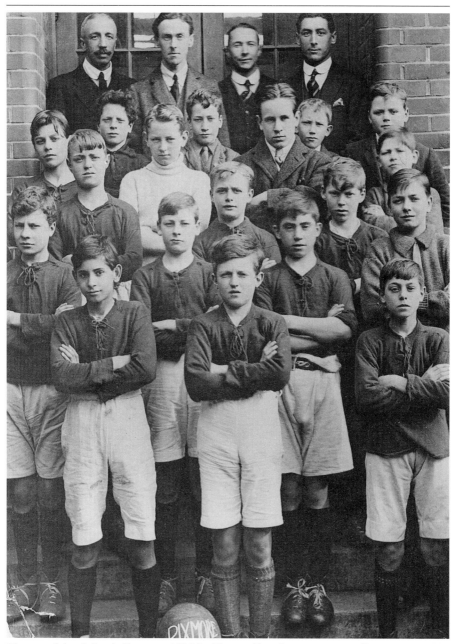

Pixmore School football team, 1920/1. The staff and team are: (staff) Mr Horn, Mr Varley, Mr Shingler, Mr Simpson; (team) Bob Garrat, T. Rowley, George Angel, Albert Morrad, Jack Wilkinson, Chris Chapman, Alfred Williams, Ernie Johnson, Arthur Shenton, Chris Foster, Len Franklin, Alfie Gardner, Charlie Walker, James Cave, Tom Swain, Frank Dodge, George Wilson, Ernie Smith.

Norton Road School, Norton Road, was the first County Council school to open on the estate. This photograph shows part of the opening ceremony, which took place on 16 October 1909.

In 1937, to mark the coronation of King George VI, Letchworth schools and the Brownies planted three avenues of trees on Norton Common. Most of these, now magnificent trees, are still standing today.

Some of the children of Hillshott School enjoying a performance of *Cinderella* in the early 1950s.

Tennis at St Francis College, Broadway. This photograph is difficult to date but it could have been taken in the early 1950s.

The kindergarten at St Francis College, Broadway, in the early 1950s. In 1995 a kindergarten facility reopened at the college.

Some of the children of St Francis College happily drawing in the sunshine in the early 1950s.

Section Eight

INDUSTRY AND COMMERCE

This magnificent beast is the Duke of Puddington, who lived at Pixmore Farm and was photographed in about 1909. Pixmore Farm was managed by First Garden City Limited and was situated just off Pixmore Avenue where the Garden House Hospice is today.

Works' outings were often organized by companies. These buses are parked outside the Kosmos Photographics factory in Pixmore Avenue sometime in the early 1930s. Unfortunately the exact date or the destination is uncertain. Kosmos Photographics manufactured photographic paper and first started business in Letchworth in 1911.

Several companies had railway sidings serving their factories. This photograph, which dates from about 1932, shows books from the printers J.M. Dent and Sons being loaded at Dunhams Lane. Dents' premises are on the left, in the background is part of the Kryn and Lahy factory and to the right is the Meredews' building. The man in uniform and peaked cap in the centre of the picture is Arthur Chalkley; immediately to the right of him, wearing an apron and pushing a barrow, is Frank Bourne, and on the far right, in uniform and pushing a loaded barrow, is either Les or Sid Chalkley.

Part of the Irvin Airchute factory in the late 1920s. The company manufactured parachutes and was established in the Garden City in 1926. The man at the end of the line, on the left, is unidentified. Second from the left is Hilbert Hamer, who helped Leslie Irvin get the company started; next is Mrs Corkhill, Inspection Assistant; the unidentified gentleman standing next to her is from the Air Inspection Department; and at the front of the line is Leslie Irvin, who founded the company.

The year is 1907 and the factory under construction at the junction of Works Road and Pixmore Avenue is being built for W.H. Smith and Son, bookbinders. W.H. Smith and Son was one of the first major companies to be established in Letchworth Garden City.

W.H. Smith and Son's factory was later occupied by a number of other companies. One of these was the Morse Chain Company Limited, who manufactured precision chain drive equipment for many industries.

During the Second World War Morse Chain Company Limited products made an important contribution to the war effort, as can be seen from this promotional card of the early 1940s.

Francis & Bevan, smallholders, were situated at Woodland Cottage, Whitethorn Lane. This photograph was taken in 1913.

The Garden City had a thriving motor vehicle industry including the Lacre Motor Car Company Limited, which moved to Letchworth Garden City in 1909. Its factory was in Works Road and its products included charabancs.

One of William Auburn dairy's delivery carts in Wilbury Road, 1908. Mr Stapleton is sitting in the cart.

Mr Taylor at Kinora Limited, *c.* 1911. The Kinora system was a method of showing motion pictures in the home: it used a Kinora viewer, which contained a revolving reel of individual photographs. As each photograph came into view it was held momentarily thus giving the illusion of movement. Several reels can be seen behind Mr Taylor. Kinora Limited, which was in Pixmore Avenue, suffered a disastrous fire on 7 January 1914. Three days later a new motor fire-engine arrived for Letchworth Fire Brigade.

Disastrous fires seem to have been a speciality in Letchworth. On 2 May 1913 smoke was seen coming from the industrial area of the town and many people rushed to see what was happening. Even the shopkeepers locked up their shops and dashed to the scene. Hayes (Universal) Printing Machinery Limited, Works Road, was on fire. Although the fire brigade was called, it could do little and the buildings and much of the machinery were destroyed. The company were calico printers, using all rotary lithographic machines.

Vickers & Field, asphalt manufacturers, Works Road, was the first company to start business in the Garden City. Unfortunately the pollution produced by its manufacturing process led to complaints from nearby residents.

The Glebe Dairy was at No. 30 Glebe Road. Milk was originally delivered by hand-cart but the dairy started using motorized transport in the 1950s.

The factory of J.M. Dent and Sons, printers and bookbinders, 1907. Dents was one of the first major companies to relocate from London to the Garden City. The photograph was taken from Works Road, looking towards Dunhams Lane.

The Linotype room at Dents, 1914. Printing and publishing was an important part of the economy of the Garden City. In 1907, as well as Dents, there was the Arden Press Limited, Garden City Press Limited, W.H. Smith and Son, and Wheeler, Odell and Company.

Compositors working at the Garden City Press, *c.* 1908. The Garden City Press was founded in 1904 and occupied temporary premises in Hitchin, before moving to Pixmore Avenue in Letchworth Garden City in 1906.

One of the first companies to come to Letchworth Garden City was Heatly-Gresham Limited, engineers, who moved to new factory premises on Works Road from Bassingbourn in 1905. This photograph shows employees on a works' outing to Bedford in 1906. The men are taking a break at Old Warden, Bedfordshire.

Glass bell cloches protecting Mr Cole's lettuces. Agriculture and the promotion of smallholdings and allotments were important parts of the Garden City philosophy. It is not certain who Mr Coles was, but he may well have had a smallholding.

'The Sheds' in Nevells Road were used for a variety of industrial purposes. The Bowyer-Lowe Company Limited had its radio works here from 1923 until 1927. Bowyer-Lowe radios were exported all over the world.

The Kryn and Lahy Metal Works was started in 1915 by Belgian refugees. Its output was mainly munitions. A group of Belgian munitions workers is seen here, one holding an artillery shell. This photograph was taken in 1916 or 1917.

Shell manufacture at Kryn and Lahy during 1916.

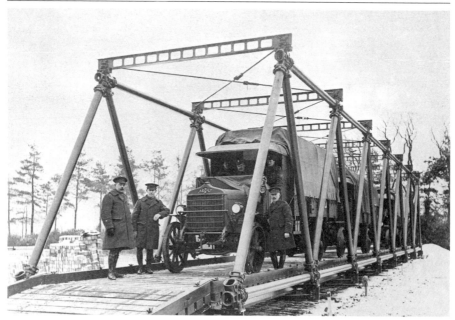

During the First World War Kryn and Lahy also manufactured the Inglis Pattern Portable Bridge. The photograph shows the rectangular pattern bridge, which first began to arrive in France early in 1917. This type was not strong enough to carry tanks and was too low for the passage of motor buses.

These buildings housed the offices, laboratory and drawing offices of Kryn and Lahy during the First World War.

A converter in action at the Kryn and Lahy factory in 1938. The group of men watching the blow-out are delegates from the engineering section of the British Association.

E. Harding's newsagents in The Wynd during the mid-1920s. Harding's also sold tobacco from a house, No. 66 Ridge Avenue. In the 1920s other small businesses were conducted from houses, including a cobbler's in Hillshott.

Marmet Prams being manufactured at the company's Icknield Way factory in the 1930s. The company was established in 1912.

This striking building on Icknield Way was the offices of the Country Gentleman's Association. The CGA could supply everything from seed potatoes to tennis rackets and aeroplanes.

The Garden City Embroidery Works was one of the first factories in the Garden City, starting business in 1905. This photograph, taken in the 1950s, shows the interior of the Lorraine Works, Works Road, with an automatic Jaquard punch machine.

The machine room at the Garden City Embroidery Lorraine Works in the 1950s.

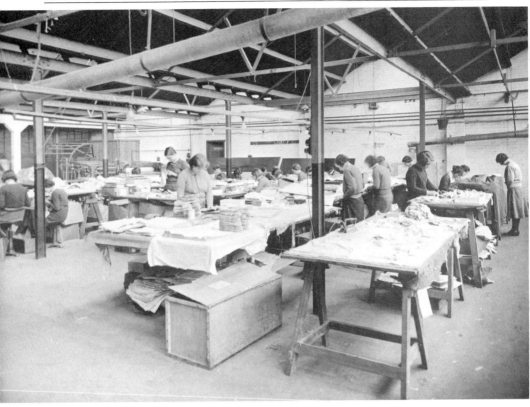

Finally the despatch department. The company's products were exported all over the world.

Milk being delivered by the Central Dairy during the First World War. The two boys holding the horses' heads were Belgian refugees; both died during the influenza epidemic of 1918.

J.C. Beale's removal lorry. Beale of Letchworth is first mentioned in the 1933/4 Letchworth Directory at No. 2a Leys Avenue. The last reference appears in the 1958/9 Directory at the same address.

The junction of Birds Hill and Pixmore Avenue, *c.* 1950. Today the roads would be crowded with cars, vans and lorries, but when this photograph was taken the bicycle was the most common vehicle. The building on the right, occupied by Cobb & Ward, builders merchants, was built in 1914 as the Tenement Factory. Part of the Nip In Café can be seen to the left. The café has a very long history dating back to about 1908; it is still there today.

Fred Nott, the baker, started his bakery on 3 March 1907 from a shop in Leys Avenue. This photograph was taken outside Nott's bakery in Commerce Avenue in the early 1950s, by which time he had several shops and restaurants.

The staff of Letchworth Bacon Company, 1936. The company was formed in the previous year to operate the model abattoir. In the 1950s Letchworth Bacon Company processed about 4,000 animals per week.

Section Nine

'PULL YOURSELVES TOGETHER GIRLS':
THE SPIRELLA COMPANY, 1910–89

In 1910 the Spirella Company of Great Britain, manufacturers of ladies' corsets, started work in Letchworth Garden City. Its first temporary premises were 'The Sheds' in Nevells Road, seen in the background of this photograph taken in 1910.

In 1913 Spirella held its first field day, with fun and games including a costumed egg and spoon race on bicycles.

Work on the permanent factory began in 1912, with the wing nearest the railway being constructed first. The builders were Henry Hurst of Letchworth.

By March 1913 the first wing was nearing completion and screed was being applied to the floors.

Another wing of the factory nearing completion. The large windows let in considerable amounts of daylight to the work areas.

A view of the factory from Broadwater Avenue, 1914. The statue of Sappho is in the foreground (see p. 96).

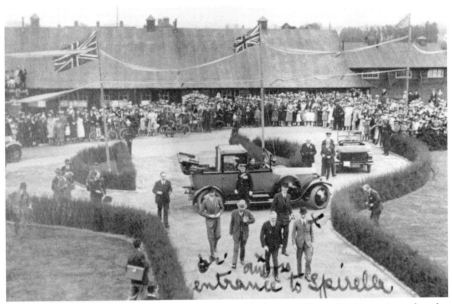

In June 1926 the Duke of York visited the Spirella factory. He arrived wearing a bowler hat and carrying an umbrella, and is seen here walking towards the entrance to the building.

One of the workrooms in the early 1920s.

The twenty-first anniversary of the foundation of the company in Letchworth Garden City took place in 1931 and was a time of great celebration. Various speeches were given, including one by Mr Brunt, seen here, and a tea party was also held.

The coronation of George VI in 1937 was celebrated by decorating the building with flags and bunting and by having it floodlit.

During the Second World War a Home Guard unit was recruited to protect the factory.

There was a spotter's post on the roof to detect enemy aircraft. If any were seen the bell would be rung very loudly.

Tea breaks for the workers were very important.

Entertainment was also provided. This is Jack Warner entertaining the employees during a BBC broadcast of *Workers' Playtime* in January 1945.

The early 1950s saw the company expanding and taking on extra staff. These are new recruits in August 1950. Back row, left to right: Kathleen Warman, Pamela Tomkies, Mrs A. Evitt, Mrs V. Redman, Sally Fraser, Nancy Harvey, Pamela Goldsmith, Janet Shepherd, Mrs T. Lawson, Joan Wright, Mrs E. Jeffs. Marjorie Houghton, Shirley Wilson. Front row: Gwendoline Cooper, Amy Ingrey, Brenda Abnett, Jean Tebbutt, Diana Gow, Margaret Cook, Kathleen Freeston, Joselyn Dear, Bessie Game, Valerie Field. Centre front: Mr Edmond and John Troy.

As new staff were recruited, old staff left. This is Miss Gladys Hudson's retirement party in June 1959. Miss Hudson started in the company in 1910 and retired as manager of the Order of Examination Department.

New styles of corset were produced. This is the corselette 'Escapade', which was introduced in 1957.

Section Ten

GARDEN CITY SCENES

Station Way at the junction with Broadwater Avenue, *c.* 1920. In the fenced triangle of land is a statue of the Greek poetess Sappho, by the sculptor Thomas Maclean. Sappho has had a rather mobile life in Letchworth. First situated in Lytton Avenue in 1907, she was quickly moved to the junction of Lytton Avenue and Meadow Way. By 1914 she had been moved again, this time to Broadwater Avenue where she stayed until 1936, when she was placed in the Ball Memorial Gardens. Here she has remained, apart from a brief adventure in 1991 when she was stolen but quickly recovered and replaced.

Norton village had a number of ponds, most of them now filled in and built over. This pond, photographed here in 1904, was the scene of a commotion in the early years of this century when loud screams were heard one night. The villagers rushed out thinking that a murder was taking place. In fact a woman, wandering home after an evening at the Three Horseshoes, had fallen in the pond. She was later fined for being drunk.

Part of Norton village in the early 1950s. St Nicholas School is on the right, beyond it is Church Lane, with St Nicholas' Church in the background.

This Christmas card, probably dating from about 1912, features one of the pre-Garden City cottages in Norton village.

The title of this photograph, taken in 1909, is Common View Road. The houses in Green Lane can be seen in the background. Common View is in the foreground and continues to the right. The left-hand road was originally known as North Fork, but was quickly renamed North Avenue. This part of Letchworth Garden City was developed with housing for people working in the nearby factories.

A rather posed group outside Letchworth Hall Hotel, c. 1907. The hotel was run by First Garden City Limited and between 25 March and 30 September 1911 full board and residence cost between 5s and £3 3s per week. The charge for visitors' servants was 30s per week.

The interior of The Arcade, 1926. The Arcade was built in 1922.

Norton Common comprises 66 acres of public open space near the centre of the Garden City. When this photograph was taken, possibly in the early 1920s, most of the common was relatively unmanaged.

The label with this photograph reads 'Bullmore's House', but the house is actually named Flaxley and is situated in Willian. A.W.E. Bullmore was resident engineer for First Garden City Limited and was one of the very first people to move to the Garden City estate, arriving in April 1904. By 1909, when this photograph was taken, the Bullmore family were living at Flaxley. Presumably the two girls with the teddy bear are the Bullmores' children.

An early view, *c.* 1907, of the junction of Birds Hill (in the foreground) with Station Road (behind) and Norton Way South (running from left to right). The children are queuing to buy a Brolia pure ice. The building to the left is the Garden City Hotel, the greenhouse in Station Road is part of W.A. Brown's nursery and further up Station Road are the Letchworth Refreshment Rooms.

Letchworth Lane in the late 1920s, with the buildings and haystacks of Letchworth Hall Farm and the sixteenth-century cottages of Letchworth village on the right.

This is also Letchworth Lane, but this time at the Hitchin Road junction end. The school sign refers to St Christopher School. The date is the early 1950s.

Meadow Way, in a view looking towards Broadway, *c.* 1912.

Eastcheap in the late 1930s, the Nott's Café to the right. Motor vehicles were common by this date but horse-drawn carts were still to be seen.

Nearing completion in early 1913 is Letchworth station, photographed from the Spirella factory roof. To the right can be seen part of the temporary station, which opened in 1905. Behind it is the wooden footbridge which was replaced by Neville Bridge in 1930.

Letchworth station in the 1930s, with packaged prams from the Marmet factory stacked outside the parcels office awaiting despatch. The permanent station opened in 1913, replacing the temporary wooden station sited a short distance down the line to Hitchin.

The loading bay at Letchworth station, photographed probably in 1929 or 1930. The men standing in front of the cart are, left to right, unknown, Reg Davies, unknown, Mr Baxter, Mr Kind, Mr Newall (who was based in Hitchin), unknown, Mr A.W. Chalkley.

Eastcheap, photographed from Letchworth Library in the early 1970s. Arena Parade, looking as though it has been transported from Stevenage New Town, is on the left. On the right a fire-engine can be seen outside the fire station.

A winter's day at Willian, in a view looking towards Roxley Court in the early 1950s.

The newly completed Letchworth Urban District Council Town Hall on Broadway, 1935. In the background the steel skeleton of the Broadway Cinema is taking shape. Both buildings were designed by the Letchworth architects Bennett and Bidwell.

Letchworth Garden City once had three cinemas, the Palace, the Broadway and the Rendezvous. This photograph, taken in 1936, shows the Broadway and Palace Cinemas. Surprisingly no photographs seem to exist of the Rendezvous Cinema, which was in Norton Way South. The Broadway Cinema is the only one surviving today.

Broadway, in a view looking north towards the railway line. A crop is being cut to the left and on the skyline just beyond the two trees can be seen Barclays Bank under construction. This dates the photograph to 1908. Also on the skyline to the right of the track is the single-storey building that was the offices of First Garden City Limited.

Leys Avenue in the snow, sometime between 1908 and 1909.

Leys Avenue, in a view looking towards Station Place in the late 1920s. To the right is T. Brooker and Sons' hardware shop with the entrance to The Arcade. Next to it is Tilley Bros, drapers and milliners, Goldhawk and Hale, corn chandlers, Underwood Bros, household stores and furnishings, 'Irene', dressmakers, and Fleming Reid & Company, hosiers.

This is not a very clear photograph but it does show how close the urban part of the Garden City estate was to its agricultural belt. The flock of sheep are being driven along Baldock Road, a sight that was probably not unusual when the photograph was taken in about 1910, but which today would create great interest, if not chaos.

Development of the Garden City was piecemeal, as can be seen from this photograph taken in 1907. The scene is Leys Avenue and shows how few shops had been built. Many residents had to walk to Hitchin or Baldock to do their shopping.

Station Way, in a view looking towards Station Place in the 1920s. To the right is Barclays Bank, and beyond it the estate office of First Garden City Limited. Part of Leys Avenue and The Colonnade can also be seen.

Station Road shops, 1908 or 1909. Included in this parade of shops are, from the left, Ben Hawkes, clothier, Jensen and Milne, florists, nurserymen and seedsmen, W. Rogers and Son, boot and shoe makers and dealers, H.E. Williams, jewellers, A.W. Page, cycle agents and assurance agent, and P. Beddoes, tobacconists and confectioners.

The Tenants' Hall, which opened on 13 March 1908, was the social centre for the Garden City Tenants, Pixmore Estate. The original building, seen in this photograph taken in about 1909, was extended in 1912. The hall, soon renamed the Pixmore Institute, was used for performances of the Garden City pantomines in 1909, 1910 and 1911. It was also the venue for the inquest into the murder of Margaret Young, aged two months. Her body was discovered buried on an allotment next to the railway in March 1910. The Pixmore Institute is now Hillshott School.

The Pixmore Institute was a venue for visiting groups in the early years of the Garden City. Here a group from the Co-operative movement pose by the entrance in 1909. Ebenezer Howard, the founder of the garden city movement and Letchworth Garden City itself, is standing in the front row, holding his coat, third from the right. Howard was disappointed that the Co-operative movement did not have a more dynamic effect on the development of Letchworth Garden City.

The charmingly named Style House consisted of the shops Discerna and the Metro for Ladies Hairdressing, and was sited in Station Road near the junction with Station Place. Discerna is first listed in the 1935 Directory and had closed by the 1950s. The photograph was taken probably in the late 1930s.

The caption for this photograph, taken in about 1908, reads Baldock Road. In fact this is Hitchin Road. Today it is a busy through route, quite a contrast to the almost deserted road seen here.

Road-making in Letchworth Lane, *c.* 1925.

Two delivery vehicles in Jackmans Place, sometime in the late 1920s or early 1930s. The horse-drawn cart in the foreground is delivering milk and the motor lorry behind is delivering beer from Flittons brewery in Stotfold. Perhaps the story is true that Letchworth folk had their beer delivered to their doorsteps with their milk because there were no pubs.

Guysfield, a substantial detached residence on the edge of Willian village, was built in about 1884. It was incorporated into the Garden City estate in 1903. This photograph was taken about 1905. Today Guysfield is a private residential home for the elderly.

This photograph is something of a mystery. At first glance it is simply a view of Campers Road, which was built in 1915. On closer inspection two flag-poles can be seen in gardens to the left and others can be faintly seen in the background. Why are they there? A possible clue is that this part of Letchworth was known as 'Little Antwerp' because of the large numbers of Belgian refugees living there during the First World War. Are the flag-poles there to celebrate the end of that war?

The village of Norton has one pub, the Three Horse Shoes, pictured here in the late 1930s. There has been a public house on this site for at least 200 years. In 1834 Norton Village School started in a room in the public house.

This is Hillshott just before the First World War. The road is very busy with two horse-drawn delivery carts, a horse-drawn cart selling ice-cream to the left and in the background, to the right, a hand-cart with a milk churn. In the distance can be seen the Pixmore Institute.

Hillshott again, but this time in a view looking towards Norton Way South in the 1930s. At the end of the road can be seen the first Free Church.

Letchworth Hospital, 1931. Fund-raising for the hospital was started in 1914 but the outbreak of war intervened and the Pixmore Farm House was used as a temporary hospital. In 1920 over £5,000 was raised and the foundation stone laid in January 1921. On 15 October 1921 HRH The Princess Beatrice opened the hospital, which was partly financed by public subscription.

In the early years of the Garden City conditions were very difficult, particularly in wet weather, as much of the town centre was one large building site. Few roads were made up and the pavements consisted of a layer of cinders. This is Leys Avenue in 1907 and the unfinished condition of the road and pavement is clear.

In the 1920s Leys Avenue was one of the major shopping streets where you could buy everything, from hardware at Brookers to headache cures from Boots the Chemists.

Birds Hill, *c*. 1906. In the background are Silver Birch Cottages in Station Road. Horse and cart was a common means of transport up to the 1920s and '30s. The name Birds Hill comes from the name of a field.

Howard Park in the 1930s, with the Mrs Howard Memorial Hall in the background. The paddling pool was built on the site of a series of boggy ponds where children would catch frogs and newts.

A tranquil Leys Avenue, almost deserted apart from the lady apparently abandoned in her bath chair. The date is about 1909. T. Brooker and Sons shop is on the left. Brookers had a business in Letchworth Garden City from almost the very beginning of the Garden City until the late 1980s.

Elegant silver birch trees flank the roadway in this 1930s view of Station Road, looking towards Howard Park Corner.

The People's House, Station Road, in the late 1920s. The manager, Bill Furmston, is standing outside. The People's House was the successor to the Skittles Inn and offered food, drink, non-alcoholic of course, and entertainment.

The Wynd was built to provide access to the rear of the shops in Station Road and Leys Avenue, and also to accommodate a number of small workshops. It was not intended to be a through route. However, some of the workshops became shops and people began to use The Wynd as a through route between Station Road and Leys Avenue. The result was that the unmade road surface became a sea of mud in bad weather and there were many complaints. The photograph dates from about 1908 and shows the rutted, but dry, surface of the road.

These two boys are standing opposite the shops in Leys Avenue on a spring day in 1908. In 1922–3 the area was developed as The Arcade, the Midland Bank and shops.

Newly completed houses in Pix Road, 1907 or 1908. Most have water butts, a common feature of many buildings in Letchworth Garden City. Pix Road was built by Garden City Tenants, a Co-Partnership Housing Association which was formed in 1905.

Station Place, in a view looking towards Eastcheap. Just visible in the background is Masons Garage and beyond it the Palace Cinema. The cars date the photograph to the 1930s.

The small parade of shops at the junction of Norton Road and Green Lane on a winter's day, looking from the fields on the opposite side of the road. It is difficult to date this photograph but it may have been taken in about 1920.

Station Place on a hot summer's day in the late 1920s. Coming along Station Road towards the camera is an open-top omnibus. Passengers travelling to Hitchin, or returning from Letchworth, had to duck when the bus went under the railway bridge in Cambridge Road, Hitchin, because the bridge was so low.

In 1971 demolition started for the redevelopment of Commerce Avenue, Commerce Lane and part of Gernon Road, where a new shopping centre, multi-storey car park and Council offices were to be built. Among the shops and businesses that were demolished were R.W. Smith Limited and Minnie Brown in Commerce Avenue (above) and Whiteheads Garage Limited (below).

Nortonbury Farm is situated just north of Norton village. This bleak wintery scene was photographed in the early 1950s.

Leys Avenue was a favourite subject for photographers. This view, of about 1928, is looking towards Station Place, with E. Spinks, drapers, on the right.

The railway line physically divided the Garden City estate and also divided it politically. Conservative political activity was concentrated south of the railway at the Conservative Club, seen here, and at the Howard Hall. Socialist activity was prevalent to the north of the railway and centred on the Skittles Inn. The Conservative Club opened on 17 December 1908. It is still standing and is located at the junction of Birds Hill and Rushby Mead.

In this view, taken in the 1950s, Broadway runs from left to right, with the Pixmore Way junction to the right. Letchworth Museum is on the left and in the background the flat-roofed Madonna School can be seen. The Roman Catholic church of St Hugh of Lincoln was built on the corner plot in the early 1960s.

This is Norton Way South, in a view looking north from Baldock Road, *c.* 1906. Ebenezer Howard lived in the second house from the left from 1905 until 1911.

First Garden City Limited estate office in Broadway, *c.* 1908. In 1913 enlarged offices were built in front of this single-storey building.

Broadway in 1913, showing the recently completed post office with the estate office of First Garden City Limited just beyond it to the right. In the background the railway station is under construction.

The town centre, 1930s. The view looks across Station Place with an open-top bus, and shows, from left to right, parts of Station Road, Leys Avenue and Eastcheap.